Contents

1. Feelings

A Words to Know

Highlight the words you know.

Target Words

angry	bored	confused	disappointed
embarrassed	excited	happy	jealous
lonely	nervous	sad	satisfied
scared	surprised	worried	

B Character Faces

See different facial expressions. Look and write.

①

②

③

④

⑤

⑥

1. _ x _ i _ ed

2. s _ rp _ _ _ _ _ _

3. _ _ ba _ _ a _ _ ed

4. s _ _ r _ _

5. _ ea _ _ _ _

6. _ _ _ a _ _ oin _ _ _

C Good or Bad

Categorize the feelings. Find and write.

1.

2.

Word Bank

happy   angry   scared   excited   worried   satisfied

D Scene Pictures

Guess the feelings. Look, match, and write in lowercase.

1.

2.

3.

4.

SAD

LONELY

ANGRY

BORED

E Jumbled Feelings

Rearrange the feeling words. Unscramble and write in lowercase.

1. S D A

2. E S C F N O U D

3. J S O E A L U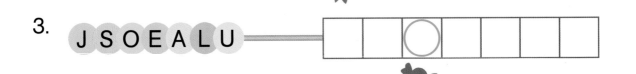

4. S U N V O E R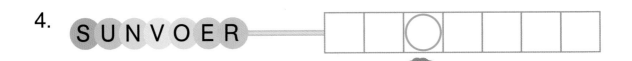

5. Y L O L E N

6. E D E X C T I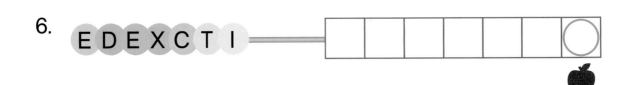

Write the letters that are circled.

He looks ____ ____ ____ ____ ____ ____!

I am happy to know you.

 A **Happy Valentine's Day**

Nick and Nora are enjoying a happy Valentine's Day.
Read, circle, and number.

"Happy Valentine's Day!"
"I am | worried | happy |
to know you."

"Let's make cupcakes."
"Great! I'll help you out."

"Today is Valentine's Day!
I want to do something for
my friends."

4

"I made some for you, too."
"I am | happy | angry |
to have you for my brother."

 B **Write Right!**

Unscramble and write.

I   am   know   you.   happy   to

2. Health

A Words to Know

Highlight the words you know.

Target Words

bandage	bruise	cast	cold	cough
cut	fever	flu	hurt	itch
medicine	pain	sick	sneeze	
headache	toothache	stomachache		
broken arm	runny nose	sore throat		

B Ache Ache!

See the people in pain. Look and write.

1. f __ __

2. __ __ t

3. i __ __ __

4. __ __ __ __ __ ache

5. b __ u __ s __

6. tooth __ __ __ __

C Hospital Chart

Find Rachel's symptoms on the chart. Look, check, and trace.

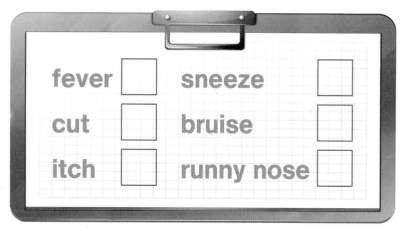

fever ☐   sneeze ☐

cut ☐   bruise ☐

itch ☐   runny nose ☐

D Two in One

Make the words. Read, write, and match.

1.		=	
2.	+ ache	=	
3.		=	
4.	sore +	=	
5.	runny +	=	
6.	broken +	=	

E Shadows in the Hospital

Meet the sick shadow men. Look and write.

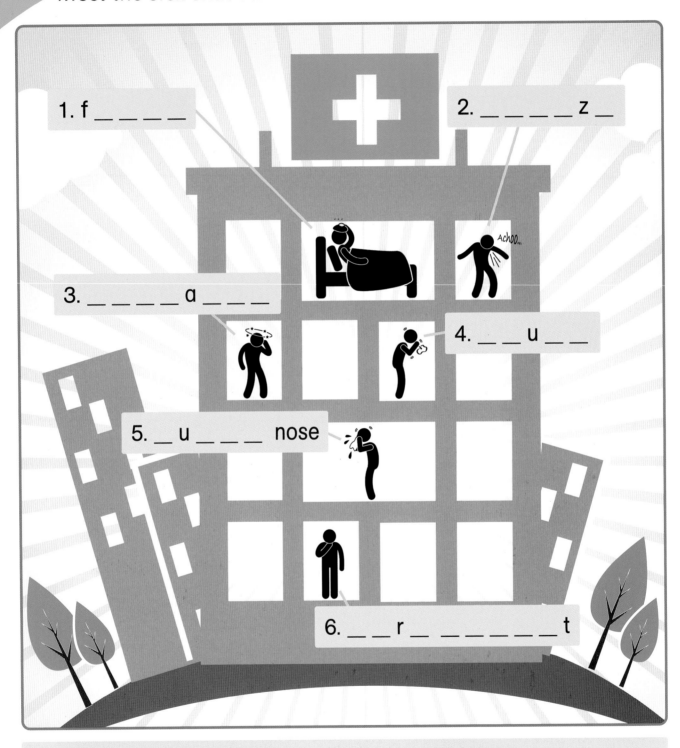

1. f _ _ _ _

2. _ _ _ _ _ z _

3. _ _ _ _ _ a _ _ _ _

4. _ _ u _ _

5. _ u _ _ _ nose

6. _ _ r _ _ _ _ _ _ t

These are c _ _ _ symptoms!

Words in Use

I have a stomachache.

 A **Bobby's Awful Day**

Bobby can't get out of bed. Read and circle the sickness words.

1.

My stomach hurts.
I have a stomachache.

2.

I have a cold.
I have a cough.

3.

I can't stop all of these sneezes.
I need some medicine.

 **B** **Read Again!**

Complete the sentence.

One day, Bobby can't get out of bed.
"My stomach hurts. _____"

Day 5

A Mirror, Mirror

See the faces on the mirrors. Find and write.

□	●	★	▩	♠	◑	△	♫	♥	▣	◆	♪	♣
s	r	u	i	w	a	t	e	d	f	p	b	o

1.

I am __ __ __ __ __ .
　　♪ ♣ ● ♫ ♥

2.

I am __ __ __ __ __ __ __ __ __ .
　　□ ★ ● ◆ ● ▩ □ ♫ ♥

3.

I am __ __ __ __ __ __ __ .
　　♠ ♣ ● ● ▩ ♫ ♥

4.

I am __ __ __ __ __ __ __ __ __ .
　　□ ◑ △ ▩ □ ▣ ▩ ♫ ♥

B Angry Letters

Calm down the letters. Unscramble and write twice.

1. n v e s o u r

   _____   _____

2. j s u l o a e

   _____   _____

3. c s f u o e n d

   _____   _____

C Cause & Effect

Look what happens to Simon. Find and write.

1.

Simon falls and his head _____s.

Simon has a _____.

2.

Simon falls and gets a _____ on his ankle.

The doctor wraps Simon's ankle with a _____.

3.

Simon falls and _____s his arm.

The doctor puts Simon's arm in a _____.

Word Bank

cast   bruise   break   bandage   headache   hurt

3. Numbers

A Words to Know

Highlight the words you know.

Target Words

first	second	third	fourth
fifth	sixth	seventh	eighth
ninth	tenth	eleventh	twelfth
twentieth	thirtieth	fortieth	fiftieth
a hundred	a thousand	a million	

Day 1

B Race Track

Watch the race. Look and write.

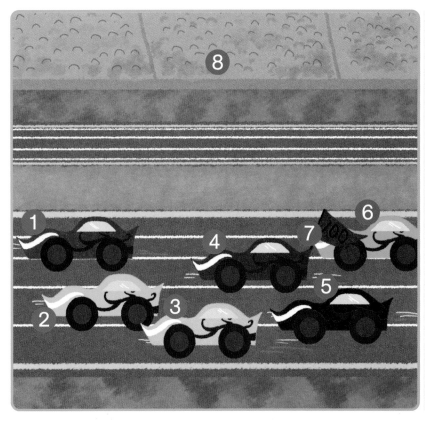

1. _ i _ st

2. s _ c _ _ _

3. _ _ i _ d

4. f _ ur _ _

5. f _ f _ _

6. _ _ xth

7. a _ _ _ _ red

8. a _ _ ou _ _ _ d

Friendly Neighbors

Visit your neighbors on different floors. Read and write.

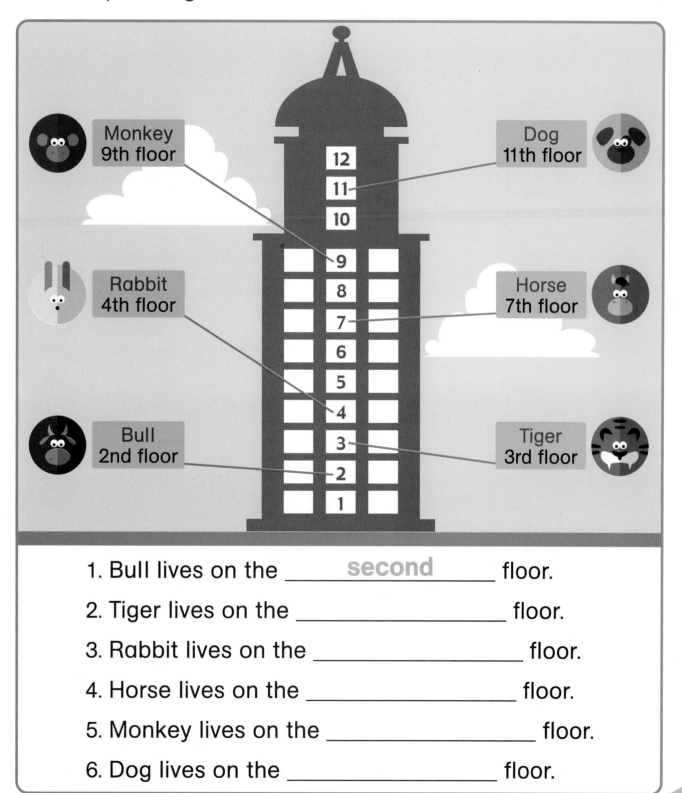

1. Bull lives on the _____second_____ floor.

2. Tiger lives on the _____ floor.

3. Rabbit lives on the _____ floor.

4. Horse lives on the _____ floor.

5. Monkey lives on the _____ floor.

6. Dog lives on the _____ floor.

D Giant Sandwich

Make a giant sandwich. Look and trace.

1. Bacon is **twelfth**.

2. Onion is **tenth**.

3. Ham is **eighth**.

4. Tomato is **fifth**.

5. Cheese is **third**.

6. Bread is **first**.

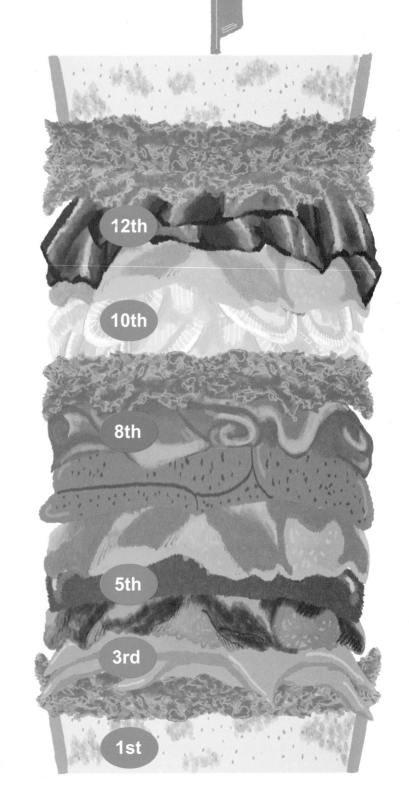

First, I see one apple tree.

 ## A A Trip to the Park

Sara sees lots of things in the park. Read and number.

First, I see one apple tree.
Second, I see two birds.
Third, I see three dogs.

 ## B Write Right!

Unscramble and write.

| I | see one | apple | First, | tree. |

4. Daily Routine

A Words to Know

Highlight the words you know.

Target Words

get up	wash one's face	brush one's teeth
take a shower	comb one's hair	get dressed
have breakfast	have lunch	have dinner
do exercise	do one's homework	do the dishes
set the table	watch TV	make one's bed
go to school	go to bed	

B Time Chart

Think about the time chart. Look and write.

 morning   afternoon   evening

1.

get up

2.  b

do one's homework

3.

make one's bed

4.

have lunch

5.

get dressed

6.

go to bed

C Schedule Board

Connect each picture to the right words. Match and trace.

watch	have	wash	take
one's face	TV	a shower	breakfast

D My Schedule

Fill in the words and mark when you do each activity.
Look and write.

1. _____ my teeth

2. _____ my hair

3. _____ _____ school

4. _____ my homework

5. _____ dinner

6. _____ _____ bed

E Confused Kids

Help the kids to find what they need to do.
Look, match, and write.

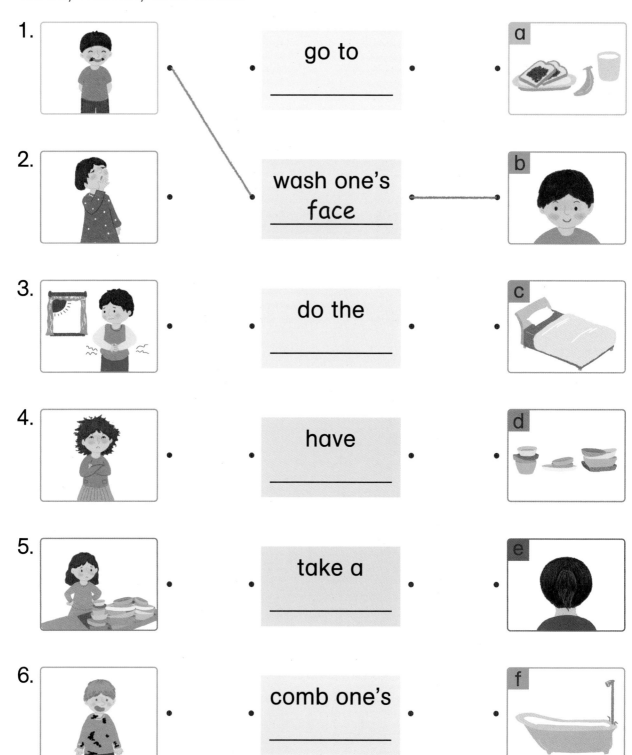

1.

go to
_____

a

2.

wash one's
face

b

3.

do the
_____

c

4.

have
_____

d

5.

take a
_____

e

6.

comb one's
_____

f

Day 4

I get dressed for school.

 A **Busy Morning**

Ben is busy in the morning. Look and choose.

1.

a	I get dressed for school.
b	I take a shower.
c	I do my homework.

2.

a	I eat dinner.
b	I go to school.
c	I brush my teeth.

B **Write Right!**

Unscramble and write.

| I | for | school. | dressed | get |

A   Ben's Day

Help him write his diary. Look, read, and write.

1.

In the morning, after I _____ _____ I do many things. First, I get _____.

2.

_____, I have breakfast. Then I _____.

3.

Third, after school I do my _____. My family has _____ together.

4.

_____, I read a story with my little sister. Then, I go _____ _____.

Word Bank

get up	dinner	to bed	dressed
Second	Fourth	homework	go to school

B   Number Patterns

Figure out the pattern of the numbers. Read and write.

1. first — _____ — _____ — fourth — fifth

2. second — fourth — _____ — _____ — tenth

Day 5

C Maze Match Up

Follow the correct path to match the words and pictures.
Find and write.

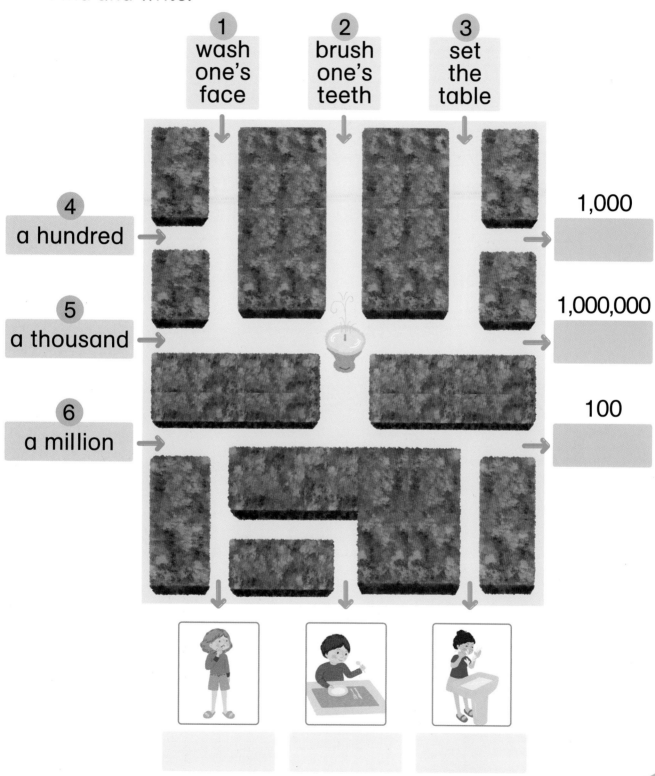

1 wash one's face

2 brush one's teeth

3 set the table

4 a hundred

5 a thousand

6 a million

1,000

1,000,000

100

5. House

A Words to Know

Highlight the words you know.

Target Words

attic	ceiling	chimney	door	fence
fireplace	floor	garage	garden	gate
kitchen	roof	stairs	study	wall
window	bathroom	bedroom	dining room	living room

B Inside the House

Visit the four-story house. Look and write.

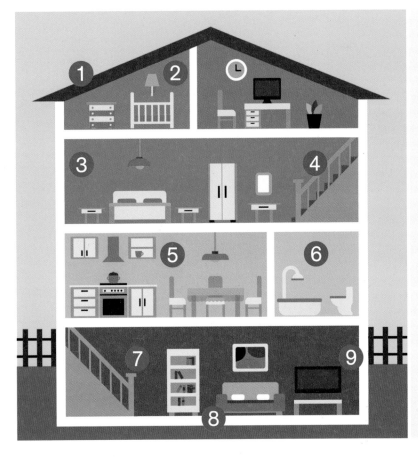

1. r __ __ f

2. at __ i __

3. b __ __ room

4. st __ __ rs

5. ki __ ch __ n

6. b __ __ __ r __ __ m

7. __ __ __ ing r __ __ __

8. fl __ __ __

9. __ __ ll

C Village Tour

See many different houses in the village. Find, write, and trace.

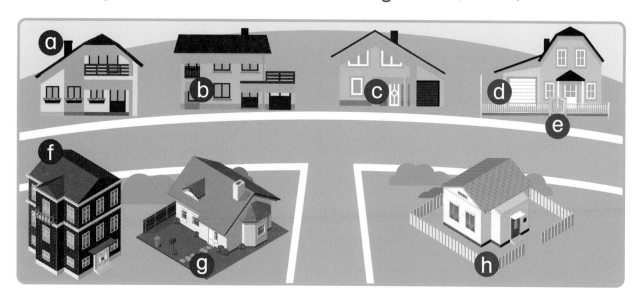

1.	**gate**	2.	**roof**	3.	**door**	4.	**fence**
	e						

5.	**window**	6.	**chimney**	7.	**garden**	8.	**garage**

D My Apartment

Visit my apartment. Look and write.

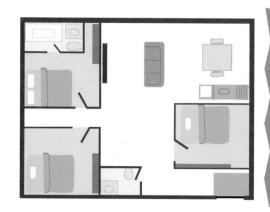

There are three 1. b_____s,

one 2. l_____ _____, one

3. k_____, and two

4. b_____s in my apartment.

E House Repair

Find out what you want to fix. Look, circle, and write.

1.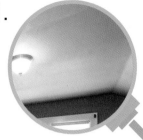

roof

ceiling

chimney

2.

window

chimney

floor

3.

door

fence

ceiling

4.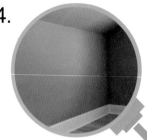

gate

wall

fireplace

5.

gate

window

stairs

6.

garage

garden

kitchen

Repair Plan

I want to fix the 1._____, the 2._____,

the 3._____, the 4._____,

the 5._____, and the 6._____.

Day 2

I can hide in the living room.

A Hide-and-seek

Ben and Julia are playing hide-and-seek. Find and write.

I can hide in the 1. _____.

I can hide in the 2. _____.

I can hide in the 3. _____.

I can hide in the 4. _____.

Let's get started. I'll count to ten.

Word Bank

kitchen	bathroom	living room	dining room

B Write Right!

Unscramble and write.

living room.	in	I	can hide	the

6. Things in the House

A Words to Know

Highlight the words you know.

Target Words

air conditioner	bed	blanket	bookcase
clock	closet	curtain	dresser
lamp	mirror	pillow	remote control
shelf	sofa	table	television
tissue	toilet	toilet paper	

B Household Items

See what's in the room. Read and circle the pictures.

> I see a bed, a pillow, a lamp, a clock, a mirror, and a bookcase.

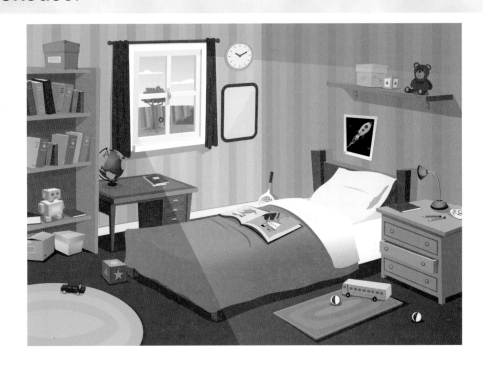

C Missing Objects

Help Julia find things in the house. Find and write.

1. She is looking for the blanket under the table. ☐

2. She is looking for the tissue behind the television. ☐

3. She is looking for the remote control behind the sofa. ☐

a

b

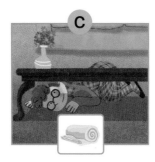
c

D Amazing Aquarium

See the words in the fish tank. Look and count.

1. shelf ☐   2. dresser ☐   3. toilet ☐   4. curtain ☐

E Scavenger Hunt

Find the differences between the two pictures.
Find, circle, and write twice in alphabetical order.

lamp

television

toilet paper

clock

blanket

mirror

bookcase

dresser

1. _____ _____ 2. _____ _____

3. _____ _____ 4. _____ _____

5. _____ _____ 6. _____ _____

Put your clothes in the closet.

A Messy Room

Mother is asking Mark to clean up his messy room.

1.

You need to clean your
messy _____.
Put your clothes in the
_____.

2.

Make your _____
and clean up your
desk. Then mop up
the _____.

Word Bank

closet   bed   room   floor

B Read Again!

Your clothes are lying all over the floor. What would your mother say to you?

_____ your clothes _____.

A Picture Pairs

Look and write the missing words. Find and write.

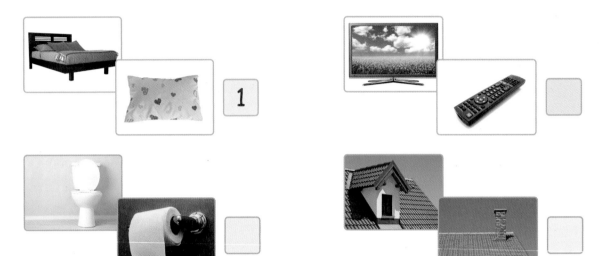

1. bed — ____

2. roof — ____

3. television — ____

4. toilet — ____

B Word Match

Make the name of each household item. Match and write.

1. remote • • conditioner ═══ ____

2. toilet • • control ═══ ____

3. air • • paper ═══ ____

C House Things

Fill in the empty house. Find and write.

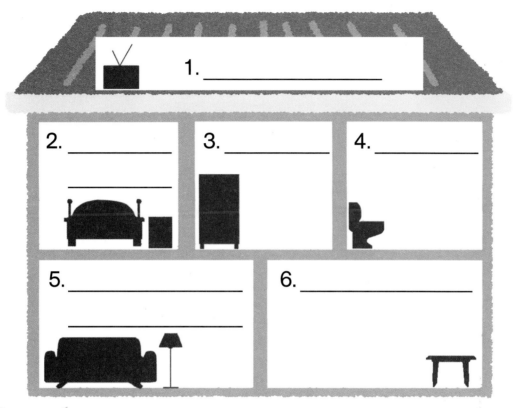

1. _____

2. _____
   _____

3. _____

4. _____

5. _____
   _____

6. _____

Word Bank

bed	table	sofa	dresser
bookcase	toilet	lamp	television

D Odd One Out

Find the different word. Read and circle.

1. bathroom — bedroom — shelf — kitchen

2. pillow — garage — mirror — tissue

3. clock — ceiling — wall — floor

7. Hobbies

A Words to Know

Highlight the words you know.

Target Words

hobbies	collect coins	draw pictures
go hiking	go shopping	go to the movies
listen to music	play computer games	play the guitar
read books	ride a bike	surf the web
take a walk	take care of pets	take photos

B School Clubs

Find a club to join on the bulletin board. Look and write.

1. g _ _ _ the

   _ o _ _ _ _

2. _ lay the g _ i _ ar

3. li _ _ en to musi _

4. t _ ke p _ ot _ s

5. _ r _ _

   p _ _ _ _ _ _ _ _

Day 1

Word to Word

Look at the scattered words. Connect and write twice.

1.

take	care	the	pets	
go	to	of	movies	

2.

ride	the	web	
surf	a	bike	

3.

do	computer	guitar	
play	the	games	

4.

take	care	the	movies	
go	to	of	pets	

5.

take	computer	games	
play	a	walk	

6.

collect	TV	
watch	coins	

D Picture Code

Break the code to find the hobbies. Find, write, and match.

a	b	c	d	e	g	h	i	k	l	n	o	p	r	s	t	u	w	y

Day 2

1.

 • a

2.

 • b

3.

 • c

4.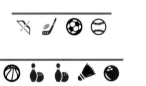

 • d

5.

 • e

Do you want to go to the movies?

 A ## Saturday Plans

Help Robin and his family decide what to do today.
Read and circle the hobbies.

Do you want to take a walk?

No, not today.

Do you want to go to the movies?

Yes, I'd love to!

 B ## Write Right!

Unscramble and write.

| go | Do | want to | you | to the movies? |

_____ movies?

8. Sports

A Words to Know

Highlight the words you know.

Target Words

sports	archery	badminton	baseball
basketball	bowling	bungee-jumping	cycling
football	golf	hockey	ice skating
ping-pong	skydiving	soccer	swimming
rock climbing	taekwondo	tennis	volleyball
water skiing	weight-lifting		

B Health Center

Join a sports team at the health center. Look and write.

1. p _ _ _ - p _ _ g

2. _ o _ l _ n _

3. w _ i _ _ _ -
   l _ f _ _ ng

4. _ _ _ mi _ to _

5. _ a _ k _ _ ball

6. s _ i _ _ in _

C Math Game

Do the math to make the sport words. Find and write.

1. cycle − e + ing

    =

2. fly + ootb − ly + all

    =

3. socks − ks + cer

    =

4. tiger − ig + nnis − r

    =

5. gate + ol − ate + f

    =

6. boat − at + wling

    =

7. vet + olley − et + ball

    =

8. ski − i + y + diving

    =

D Spilled Ink

Find the missing letters and solve the quiz.

1. arc ery
    weig t-lifting

     is letter ☐.

2. badmint 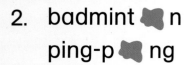 n
    ping-p  ng

     is letter ☐.

3. i 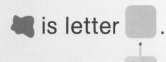 e skating
    ro k climbing

     is letter ☐.

4. s  ydiving
    water s 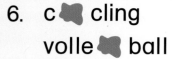 iing

     is letter ☐.

5. bask 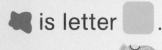 tball
    ta kwondo

     is letter ☐.

6. c 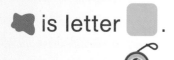 cling
    volle ball

     is letter ☐.

I love to play ___ ___ ___ ___ ___ ___!

Day 4

I love to play basketball!

 A **Sammy's Sports**

Sammy likes to play a lot of sports. Find and write.

1.

   I love to _____ _____!

2.

   _____ _____ is so fun!

3.

   _____ is the best.

Word Bank

Baseball   play basketball   Playing soccer

 B **Read Again!**

What sports does Sammy like to play?

I love to _____.

I love to _____.

I love to _____.

A Sports Equipment

Put the right equipment on the right field or court.
Match and trace.

Day 5

1.  •   • **baseball** •   •

2.  •   • **tennis** •   •

3.  •   • **soccer** •   •

4.  •   • **basketball** •   •

5.  •   • **football** •   •

6.  •   • **hockey** •   •

B Journal Entry

Fill in the missing events in the journal.
Read and number.

Today is going to be a great day.

I will 1._____ pictures

and 2._____ music first. If the

weather is nice, I will 3._____ a

walk or maybe 4. go _____.

After that, I'm going to a party.

There I will 5._____ bowling

and 6. play _____.

I can't wait to start the day!

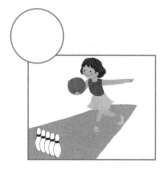

A Needle and Thread

Sew the torn clothes. Read and match.

1. I get dressed • • a one apple tree.

2. I am happy • • b for school.

3. First, I see • • c to know you.

B Write Right!

Unscramble and write.

1. a   I have   stomachache.

_____

2. I see   apple tree.   one   First,

_____

3. am happy   I   you.   to know

_____

4. play basketball!   love to   I

_____

Day 5

C Against the Wall

See the sentences on the wall. Find and write.

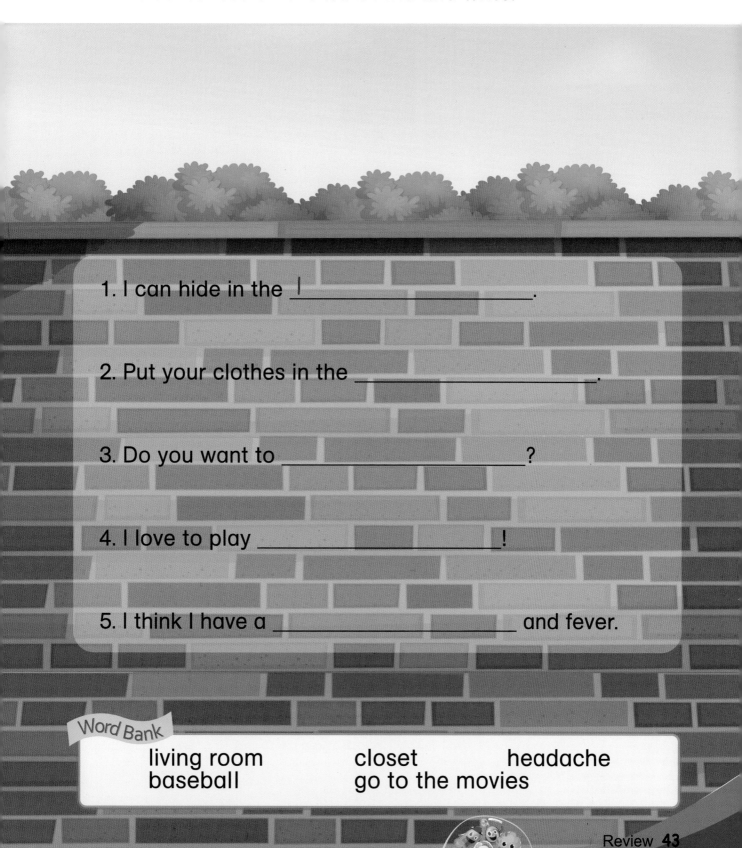

1. I can hide in the I_____.

2. Put your clothes in the _____.

3. Do you want to _____?

4. I love to play _____!

5. I think I have a _____ and fever.

Word Bank

living room   closet   headache
baseball   go to the movies

1. Feelings

p.2
B 1. excited 2. surprised
3. embarrassed 4. scared 5. jealous
6. disappointed

p.3
C 1. happy / excited / satisfied
2. angry / scared / worried
D 1. angry 2. lonely 3. sad 4. bored

p.4
E E. 1. sad 2. confused 3. jealous
4. nervous 5. lonely 6. excited / scared

p.5
A happy, happy / 3⇒2⇒1⇒4
B I am happy to know you.

2. Health

p.6
B 1. flu 2. cut 3. itch 4. headache
5. bruise 6. toothache

p.7
C fever / sneeze / runny nose
D 1. headache 2. toothache
3. stomachache 4. sore throat
5. runny nose 6. broken arm

p.8
E 1. fever 2. sneeze 3. headache
4. cough 5. runny nose
6. sore throat / cold

p.9
A hurt(s), stomachache, cold, cough,
sneeze(s), medicine
B I have a stomachache

Review(1, 2)

p.10
A 1. bored 2. surprised 3. worried
4. satisfied
B 1. nervous 2. jealous 3. confused

p.11
C 1. hurt, headache
2. bruise, bandage 3. break, cast

3. Numbers

p.12
B 1. first 2. second 3. third 4. fourth
5. fifth 6. sixth 7. a hundred
8. a thousand

p.13
C 1. second 2. third 3. fourth
4. seventh 5. ninth 6. eleventh

p.15
A 3⇒1⇒2
B First, I see one apple tree.

4. Daily Routine

p.16
B 1. a 2. b 3. a 4. b 5. a 6. c

p.17
C 1. have breakfast 2. take a shower
3. watch TV 4. wash one's face
D 1. brush 2. comb 3. go to 4. do
5. have 6. go to

p.18
E 1. wash one's face, b 2. go to bed, c
3. have breakfast, a
4. comb one's hair, e 5. do the dishes, d
6. take a shower, f

p.19
A 1. a 2. b
B I get dressed for school.

Review(3, 4)

p.20
A 1. get up, dressed
2. Second, go to school
3. homework, dinner 4. Fourth, to bed
B 1. second, third 2. sixth, eighth

p.21
C
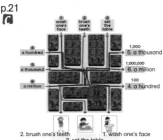

5. House

p.22
B 1. roof 2. attic 3. bedroom 4. stairs
5. kitchen 6. bathroom 7. living room
8. floor 8. wall

p.23
C 1. e 2. f 3. c 4. h 5. b 6. a 7. g 8. d
D 1. bedroom 2. living room
3. kitchen 4. bathroom

p.24
E 1. ceiling 2. floor 3. door 4. wall
5. window 6. kitchen

p.25
A 1. living room 2. bathroom
3. kitchen 4. dining room
B I can hide in the living room.

6. Things in the House

p.26
B

p.27.
C 1. c 2. b 3. a
D 1. 5 2. 2 3. 4 4. 3

p.28
E 1. bookcase 2. clock 3. dresser
4. lamp 5. mirror 6. television

p.29
A 1. room, closet 2. bed, floor
B Put, in the closet

Review(5, 6)

p.30
A 1. pillow, ,
2. chimney, ,
3. remote control, ,
4. toilet paper,
B 1. remote control 2. toilet paper
3. air conditioner

p.31
C 1. television 2. bed / dresser
3. bookcase 4. toilet 5. sofa / lamp
6. table

D 1. shelf 2. garage 3. clock

7. Hobbies

p.32
B 1. go to the movies
2. play the guitar 3. listen to music
4. take photos 5. draw pictures

p.33
C 1. take care of pets 2. ride a bike
3. play computer games
4. go to the movies
5. take a walk 6. collect coins

p.34
D 1. go hiking, d 2. draw pictures, c
3. play the guitar, a 4. read books, e
5. take photos, b

p.35
A take a walk, go to the movies
B Do you want to go to the

8. Sports

p.36.
B 1. ping-pong 2. bowling
3. weight-lifting 4. badminton
5. basketball 6. swimming

p.37
C 1. cycling, 2. football,
3. soccer, 4. tennis,
5. golf, 6. bowling,
7. volleyball, 8. skydiving,

p.38
D 1. h 2. o 3. c 4. k 5. e 6. y / hockey

p.39
A 1. play basketball
2. Playing soccer 3. Baseball
B play basketball, play soccer,
play baseball

Review(7, 8)

p.40
A 1. soccer, 2. baseball,
3. football, 4. hockey,
5. basketball,  6. tennis,

p.41
B 1. draw, 2. listen to,
3. take, 4. ice skating,
5. go, 6. computer games,

Expressions Review

p.42
A 1. b 2. c 3. a
B 1. I have a stomachache.
2. First, I see one apple tree.
3. I am happy to know you.
4. I love to play basketball!

p.43
C 1. living room 2. closet 3. go to the
movies 4. baseball 5. headache

angry

bored

lonely

scared

confused

excited

surprised

worried

jealous

nervous

satisfied

embarrassed

b __ r __ d   a __ __ ry

s __ a __ ed   l __ n __ ly

e __ c __ ted   con __ u __ ed

w __ rr __ ed   s __ rpri __ ed

n __ rv __ us   j __ __ lous

emb __ rr __ ssed   satis __ ie __

cold

cough

fever

bruise

hurt

pain

medicine

runny nose

sore throat

stomachache

headache

toothache

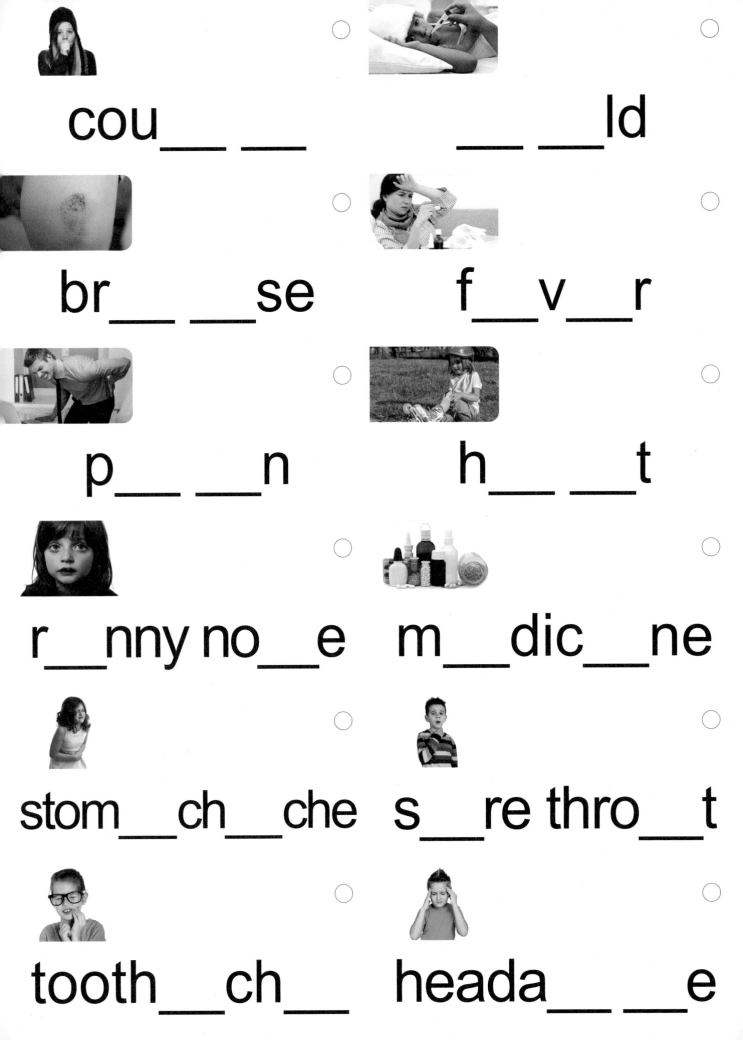

cou__ __ ⭘ __ __ __ld ⭘

br__ __se ⭘ f_v_r ⭘

p__ __n ⭘ h__ __t ⭘

r__nny no__e ⭘ m__dic__ne ⭘

stom__ch__che ⭘ s__re thro__t ⭘

tooth__ch__ ⭘ heada__ __e ⭘

first

second

third

fourth

fifth

seventh

eighth

ninth

tenth

twelfth

thirtieth

fiftieth

s __ c __ nd

__ i __ st

four __ __

t __ __ rd

sev __ n __ h

f __ __ th

ni __ __ h

ei __ h __ h

tw __ l __ th

ten __ __

fi __ ti __ th

thirt __ __ th

get up

wash one's face

brush one's teeth

get dressed

go to school

have breakfast

set the table

do the dishes

take a shower

do exercise

do one's homework

go to bed

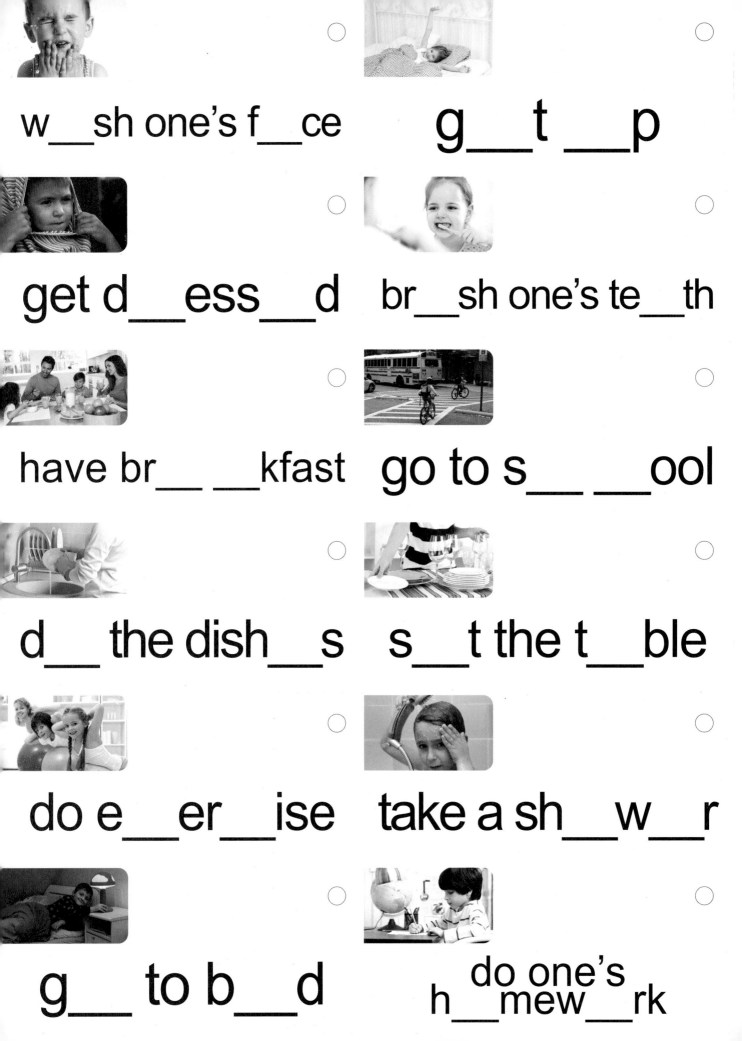

w__sh one's f__ce

g__t __p

get d__ess__d

br__sh one's te__th

have br__ __kfast

go to s__ __ool

d__ the dish__s

s__t the t__ble

do e__er__ise

take a sh__w__r

g__ to b__d

do one's
h__mew__rk

attic

bathroom

bedroom

kitchen

dining room

living room

study

garage

garden

window

roof

ceiling

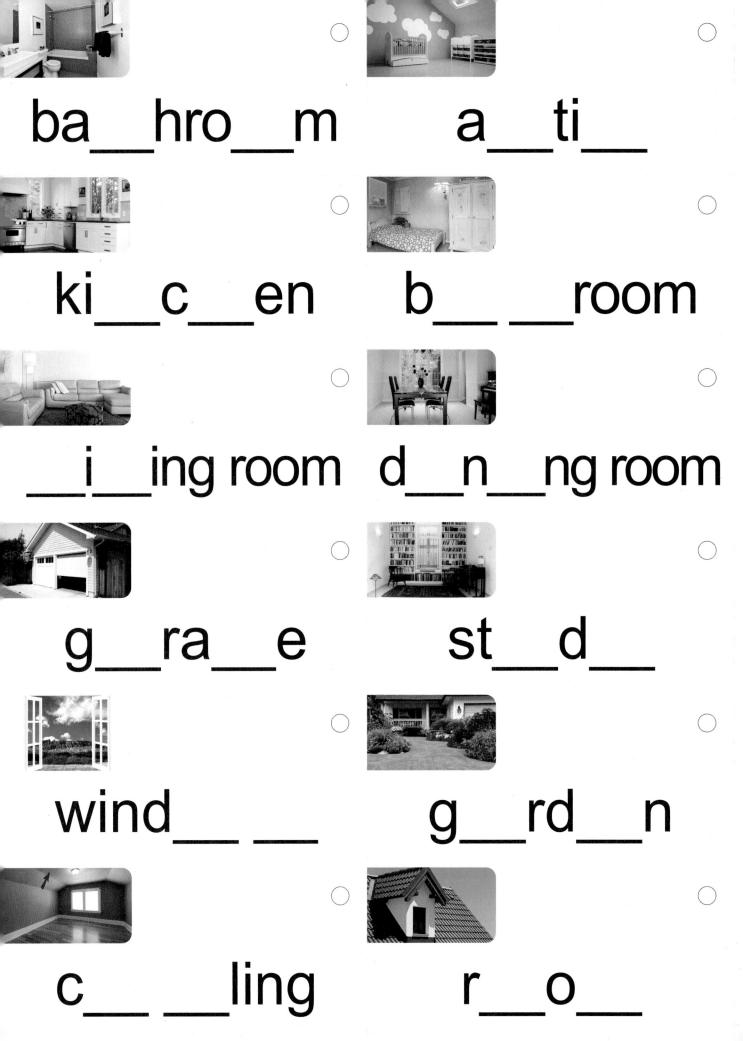

ba__ hro__ m   a__ ti__

○   ○

ki__ c __ en   b__ __ room

○   ○

__ i __ ing room   d__ n __ ng room

○   ○

g__ ra __ e   st __ d __

○   ○

wind__ __   g__ rd__ n

○   ○

c__ __ ling   r __ o __

○   ○

pillow

bookcase

closet

dresser

shelf

sofa

curtain

table

television

remote control

mirror

toilet

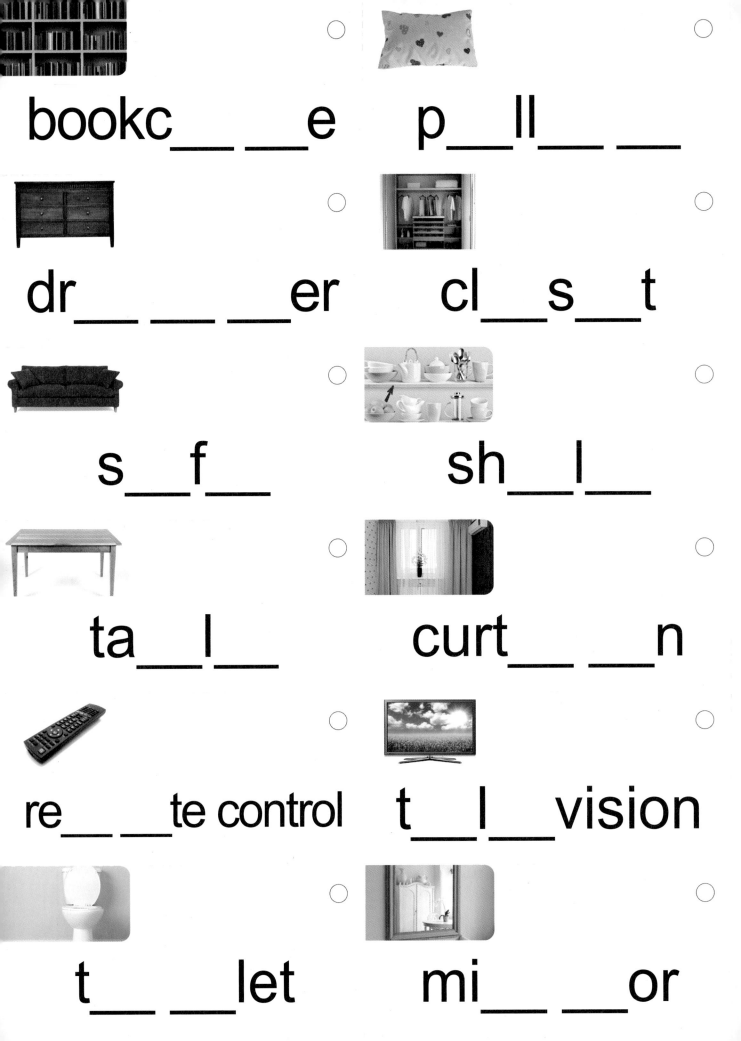

bookc_ _ _e

p_ _ll_ _ _

dr_ _ _ _er

cl_ _s_ _t

s_ _f_ _

sh_ _l_ _

ta_ _l_ _

curt_ _ _ _n

re_ _ _te control

t_ _l_ _vision

t_ _ _ _let

mi_ _ _ _or

Hobbies

draw pictures

Hobbies

go to the movies

Hobbies

take a walk

Hobbies

go shopping

Hobbies

listen to music

Hobbies

ride a bike

Hobbies

collect coins

Hobbies

read books

Hobbies

take photos

Hobbies

surf the web

Hobbies

play the guitar

Hobbies

play computer games

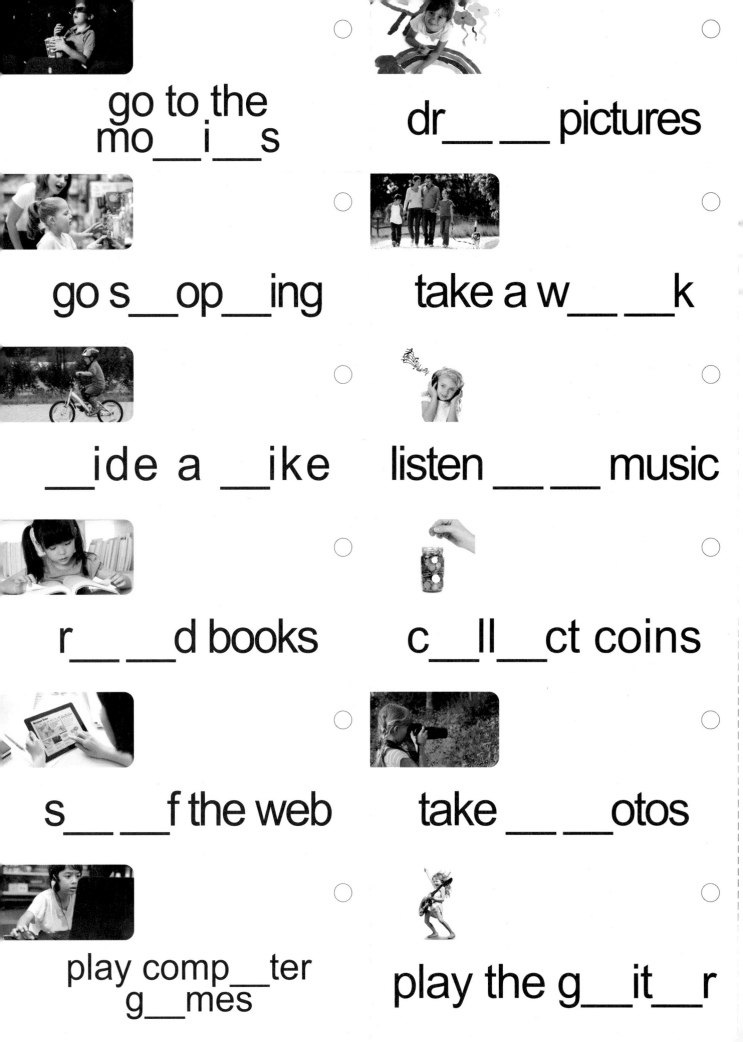

go to the mo__i__s

dr__ __ pictures

go s__op__ing

take a w__ __k

__ide a __ike

listen __ __ music

r__ __d books

c__ll__ct coins

s__ __f the web

take __ __otos

play comp__ter g__mes

play the g__it__r

Sports	Sports
baseball	basketball

Sports	Sports
soccer	ice skating

Sports	Sports
tennis	cycling

Sports	Sports
ping-pong	swimming

Sports	Sports
bowling	hockey

Sports	Sports
volleyball	badminton

ba__ __etball

ba__eb__ll

ice __ __ating

s__c__ __r

__y__ling

te__ __is

s__imm__ng

__ __ __ __ __ __ - p__ng

h__ck__y

b__ __ling

ba__ __inton

__oll__yball